THE POETRY OF RHODIUM

The Poetry of Rhodium

Walter the Educator

SKB

Silent King Books a WhichHead Imprint

Copyright © 2023 by Walter the Educator

All rights reserved. No part of this book may be reproduced in any manner whatsoever without written permission except in the case of brief quotations embodied in critical articles and reviews.

First Printing, 2023

Disclaimer
This book is a literary work; poems are not about specific persons, locations, situations, and/or circumstances unless mentioned in a historical context. This book is for entertainment and informational purposes only. The author and publisher offer this information without warranties expressed or implied. No matter the grounds, neither the author nor the publisher will be accountable for any losses, injuries, or other damages caused by the reader's use of this book. The use of this book acknowledges an understanding and acceptance of this disclaimer.

"Earning a degree in chemistry changed my life!"
- Walter the Educator

dedicated to all the chemistry lovers, like myself, across the world

CONTENTS

Dedication v

Why I Created This Book? 1

One - Oh Rhodium 2

Two - The Jewel 4

Three - Versatile Metal 6

Four - Beauty And Grace 8

Five - Eternal Sage 10

Six - Ancient Land 12

Seven - Magical Dream 14

Eight - Rearranging Their Range 16

Nine - Purging The Air 18

Ten - Advancements In Science 20

Eleven - Precious Gem 22

Twelve - Mysteries Unfold 24

Thirteen - Spark Of Inspiration		25
Fourteen - Presence Adored		27
Fifteen - Element Of Charm		29
Sixteen - Extraordinary Begins		31
Seventeen - Rhodium, A Treasure		33
Eighteen - Sparks Transformation		35
Nineteen - Enchanting Guise,		37
Twenty - Muse For Poets		39
Twenty-One - Play A Key Role		41
Twenty-Two - Depths Of Space		43
Twenty-Three - Regal Gleam		45
Twenty-Four - Wonders Of Chemistry		47
Twenty-Five - Secrets Softly Sigh		49
Twenty-Six - Gift From The Gods		51
Twenty-Seven - Radiant Alarm		53
Twenty-Eight - Shine		55
Twenty-Nine - Full Of Love		57
Thirty - Mesmerizing Element		59
Thirty-One - Forever Pristine		61
Thirty-Two - Laboratories And Jewelry		63

Thirty-Three - Power And Presence 65

Thirty-Four - Magical Defiance 67

Thirty-Five - Rings And Necklaces 69

About The Author 71

WHY I CREATED THIS BOOK?

Creating a poetry book about the chemical element rhodium was a unique and intriguing endeavor. Rhodium, with its lustrous appearance and various industrial applications, possesses a certain mystique that can inspire poetic exploration. By delving into the properties, history, and symbolism of rhodium, I can uncover new perspectives and metaphors, crafting verses that illuminate the beauty and complexity of this element. Additionally, this book can serve as an educational and artistic fusion, merging science and art to captivate readers and ignite their curiosity about the world around them.

ONE

OH RHODIUM

In the depths of Earth's embrace, a treasure lies concealed,
A metal rare and radiant, its secrets unrevealed,
Rhodium, the precious element, with luster like the moon,
A jewel among the elements, a symphony in tune.

In the heart of platinum's realm, where rarity does reside,
Rhodium claims its rightful place, with beauty bona fide,
Its silvery-white complexion, a mirror to the soul,
Reflecting light with grace and poise, its brilliance takes its toll.

From mines deep beneath the ground, where darkness cloaks its form,

Rhodium emerges, a phoenix born, a beauty to adorn,
It dances with the atoms, in a delicate ballet,
A testament to nature's art, in its own unique display.

A catalyst of change, it sparks a transformation grand,
Unlocking the potential of reactions, hand in hand,
It breathes life into molecules, igniting fiery passion,
A catalyst of progress, a catalyst of compassion.

Oh Rhodium, enigmatic element, a mystery untold,
Your presence is a testament to nature's precious gold,
As we marvel at your beauty, and the wonders that you hold,
We're reminded of the miracles, that science can unfold.

TWO

THE JEWEL

In the realm of elements, a gem does gleam,
Radiant and rare, a metal supreme.
Rhodium, oh Rhodium, with silvery-white complexion,
A mirror-like luster, a dazzling reflection.

Catalyst of change, igniting reactions,
Unlocking potential, with fiery transactions.
In laboratories of science, you hold the key,
To miracles unfurled, the wonders we can see.

Oh, precious Rhodium, a conductor of light,
Guiding us forward, through the darkest of night.
In the crucible of progress, you dance and you shine,
Transforming the ordinary, into the divine.

From catalytic converters to jewelry's embrace,
Your versatile nature leaves no trace.

A symbol of elegance, of beauty untold,
A testament to exploration's gold.
    Oh, Rhodium, how you captivate our souls,
A mesmerizing tale that science unfolds.
In your atomic structure, secrets are concealed,
Unlocking the mysteries, yet to be revealed.
    So let us marvel at your brilliance and grace,
As we venture forth, in this cosmic race.
For in the world of elements, you reign supreme,
Rhodium, the jewel that makes our dreams gleam.

THREE

VERSATILE METAL

In the realm of elements, there's a gem so rare,
A metal that dazzles, beyond compare.
Rhodium, the name, like a whisper it sings,
With beauty that soars on silvery wings.

A catalyst it is, a changer of fate,
Unleashing transformations, never too late.
In the crucible of life, it sparks the flame,
Igniting reactions, never to be the same.

Its elegance adorns, with a shimmering sheen,
A touch of sophistication, a sight to be seen.
Reflecting the world, like a mirror so bright,
Rhodium's allure, an enchanting delight.

From jewelry to engines, its talents unfold,
A versatile metal, worth more than gold.

Unlocking the mysteries, it holds the key,
Revealing hidden truths for all to see.
 In the depths of the Earth, where secrets lie,
Rhodium emerges, like a star in the sky.
A symbol of rarity, a jewel of the deep,
Its presence, a reminder, of treasures we seek.
 Oh, Rhodium, you captivate with your grace,
A precious element, in this cosmic space.
A testament to nature's endless art,
Forever etched, within the human heart.

FOUR

BEAUTY AND GRACE

In the realm of elements, a gem so rare,
Rhodium, radiant with a silvery-white glare.
A conductor of light, an elegant sprite,
Unveiling secrets, igniting the night.

An alchemist's dream, this precious metal,
Unleashing reactions, fiery and unsettled.
A catalyst of change, it dances with grace,
Awakening progress, in every space.

From catalytic converters to gleaming rings,
Rhodium's versatility forever sings.
Unlocking mysteries, it holds the key,
A symbol of exploration, for all to see.

In the depths of the Earth, it takes its birth,
Emerging with shimmering sheen, its worth.

An emblem of rarity, a treasure untold,
Captivating grace, forever etched in gold.

    A gem of transformation, a truth-revealing stone,
Rhodium's elegance, resplendently shown.
Shrouded in mystery, it captures the heart,
A precious element, never to depart.

    In the cosmic expanse, it takes its place,
Rhodium, a symbol of beauty and grace.
Forever cherished, in the depths of our soul,
A gem of wonder, that forever unfolds.

FIVE

ETERNAL SAGE

In the realm of elements, Rhodium shines bright,
A precious metal, a captivating sight.
With a luster that sparkles like the stars above,
It's a symbol of luxury, a gift from nature's trove.
    Rhodium, the catalyst of change it plays,
Unleashing reactions in mysterious ways.
A conductor of transformation, it ignites,
Unlocking secrets, bringing forth new lights.
    In the depths of the Earth, it silently lies,
Hidden in the embrace of minerals, it thrives.
Its elegance enchants, its presence enthralls,
A symbol of exploration, it beckons and calls.
    From jewelry to technology, its uses are vast,
A versatile element, forever unsurpassed.

A protector of memories, it shields with grace,
Preserving moments, leaving no trace.

Rhodium, a conductor of light divine,
Illuminating pathways, making brilliance shine.
Its captivating hues, a kaleidoscope of grace,
A treasure of the Earth, in every single trace.

Oh, Rhodium, your beauty knows no bound,
A rare gem in the alchemist's playground.
In this elemental dance, you take center stage,
A symbol of perfection, an eternal sage.

SIX

ANCIENT LAND

In the depths of the Earth, where secrets lie,
A treasure called rhodium, hidden from the eye.
A metal so rare, with beauty untold,
Its elegance shines, with brilliance unfold.

A conductor of light, it gleams with grace,
Reflecting the world, in its shimmering embrace.
A symphony of colors, a kaleidoscope of hue,
Rhodium, the maestro, painting the view.

In noble alloys, it lends its might,
Strengthens the bond, like day to night.
An element of power, it catalyzes change,
Creating new paths, where progress will range.

From jewelry to technology, it finds its place,
A catalyst for innovation, an emblem of grace.
Its versatility knows no bounds,
From rings on fingers to engines that sound.

Oh, rhodium, a symbol of exploration,
Unlocking mysteries, a source of fascination.
A treasure of the Earth, hidden and rare,
In your presence, we find wonder and flair.

So let us celebrate this element divine,
With poems and songs, with every single line.
Rhodium, a gift from nature's own hand,
A testament to the wonders of this ancient land.

SEVEN

MAGICAL DREAM

In the realm of elements, a jewel does gleam,
With brilliance untamed, a mesmerizing dream.
Rhodium, oh Rhodium, a catalyst of change,
Unfolding mysteries, secrets it'll arrange.

A metal so rare, so precious and pure,
Its beauty unmatched, forever to endure.
Silent guardian, a shimmering disguise,
Unveiling truths beneath the starlit skies.

In the lab of science, its power is unveiled,
A catalyst supreme, where reactions are hailed.
Facilitating transformation, it takes center stage,
With precision and grace, it writes a new page.

A conductor of dreams, of innovation's might,
Rhodium dances with atoms, painting colors so bright.

Unlocking the secrets, revealing what's unseen,
In its enigmatic nature, a world to convene.
 A guardian of wonders, a seeker of truth,
Rhodium's allure captivates since its youth.
From jewelry to catalysis, it blends worlds apart,
A symbol of progress, forever in our heart.
 So let us marvel at Rhodium's ethereal grace,
Its power, its beauty, a celestial embrace.
For in the realm of elements, it reigns supreme,
Rhodium, oh Rhodium, our magical dream.

EIGHT

REARRANGING THEIR RANGE

In Rhodium's realm, a mystery unfolds,
A metal rare, a story yet untold.
A lustrous beauty, elegant and bright,
Unveiling secrets in the depths of night.

Its atomic dance, a symphony so rare,
A conductor of wonders, beyond compare.
A catalyst it becomes, in chemistry's quest,
Unlocking reactions, the very best.

From jewelry's gleam to a poet's ink,
Rhodium's touch, a mesmerizing link.
A silvery whisper, a silent embrace,
Enchanting souls with its ethereal grace.

In the depths of space, where stars collide,
Rhodium's brilliance, a celestial guide.

A cosmic dance, where elements align,
Harnessing power, a force so divine.

In laboratories, where science thrives,
Rhodium's mastery, the alchemist strives.
A catalyst supreme, in the realm of change,
Transforming elements, rearranging their range.

From engines to sensors, its purpose unfolds,
Rhodium's presence, a story yet untold.
A metal rare, with versatility profound,
Unveiling mysteries, where wonders are found.

So let us celebrate this noble element,
A gift from nature, so heaven-sent.
Rhodium, we hail your elegance and might,
In every facet, you shimmer with delight.

NINE

PURGING THE AIR

In fields where wonders lie unseen,
Rhodium reigns, a sovereign of sheen.
A noble element, rare and pure,
Its allure, an enigma to endure.

In catalytic realms, it holds its might,
A catalyst of change, a beacon of light.
Transforming molecules with graceful ease,
Unlocking the secrets of chemical seas.

From automotive dreams to medical aid,
Rhodium's touch brings progress unswayed.
Cleansing emissions, purging the air,
A guardian of Earth, beyond compare.

In jewelry's embrace, it finds its place,
A precious metal, adorned with grace.

Its radiant glow, a celestial hue,
Reflecting love, forever true.

In cosmic depths, where stars collide,
Rhodium dances, a celestial guide.
Amongst the heavens, it weaves its spell,
A cosmic artist, a story to tell.

Oh Rhodium, element of grand design,
With splendor and prowess, forever shine.
In science, beauty, and realms untold,
Your wonders, Rhodium, we behold.

TEN

ADVANCEMENTS IN SCIENCE

Rhodium, the alchemist's dream,
A catalyst of change, it may seem.
In nature's laboratory, it reigns supreme,
Unleashing reactions, like a flickering beam.
    With noble grace, it takes its place,
In the realm of elements, it finds its embrace.
A silent conductor, it orchestrates,
Transforming the mundane into precious space.
    Through its touch, miracles unfurl,
Unlocking secrets, revealing a hidden world.
A guardian of wonders, it stands tall,
A silent observer, watching over all.
    Its enigmatic nature, a mystery untold,
A tale of power, yet so subtly bold.

In the depths of darkness, it silently creeps,
A protector of treasures, it safely keeps.
    Oh Rhodium, you shimmer and glow,
A radiant jewel, the heavens bestow.
In the cosmic dance, you play your part,
A star's reflection, a cosmic art.
    In laboratories and galaxies far,
You leave your mark, like a shining star.
Versatile and precious, you hold the key,
To advancements in science, for all to see.
    Rhodium, you are elegance refined,
A symbol of power, so divine.
In your presence, we find solace and grace,
A testament to the wonders of space.

ELEVEN

PRECIOUS GEM

In the realm of elements, a jewel does reside,
A shimmering metal, with secrets to confide.
Rhodium, the catalyst of change and might,
Igniting reactions, transforming the night.

In laboratories, its power does unfold,
A conductor of progress, a story yet untold.
With its atomic dance, it bends and shapes,
Creating new compounds, a world it awakes.

It glimmers in the darkness, like a cosmic ray,
A guardian of Earth, in its own mysterious way.
From catalytic converters to jewelry so rare,
Rhodium's versatility, beyond compare.

Its ethereal grace, a dream it does inspire,
Innovations born, fueled by its fire.
A bridge between worlds, it brings forth new dreams,
Unlocking possibilities, with radiant gleams.

Oh, Rhodium, enigmatic and profound,
A cosmic presence, with no limits bound.
Transforming the ordinary, into something grand,
With elegance and power, it rules the land.

So let us celebrate, this element divine,
A protector of treasures, a marvel that shines.
In the depths of its mystery, the beauty lies,
Rhodium, a precious gem, that never dies.

TWELVE

MYSTERIES UNFOLD

In the realm of elements, a gem unfolds,
Rhodium, enigmatic and profound,
A guardian of Earth, its secrets it holds,
Transforming the ordinary into something grand.

With noble prowess, it takes its stand,
In catalytic converters, it finds its place,
Cleaning the air, a touch so grand,
Rhodium's power, the world does embrace.

But beyond its practicality, it shines,
In jewelry's embrace, it captures hearts,
Elegance and power, a union divine,
Rhodium's allure, a work of art.

No limits bound, its mysteries unfold,
A precious gem that never dies,
Enduring beauty, a story untold,
Rhodium, eternal in our eyes.

THIRTEEN

SPARK OF INSPIRATION

In the Earth's embrace, a guardian so rare,
Rhodium, the element, with elegance and flair.
A silent protector, hidden beneath the soil,
Its presence, like a secret, only few can toil.

A symphony of atoms, woven in its core,
Rhodium's versatility, forever to adore.
A shield against corrosion, steadfast and true,
Protecting the metals, in every shade and hue.

From catalytic converters to jewelry so fine,
Rhodium's touch, a treasure, a shimmering sign.
Transforming the ordinary, into something grand,
A touch of Rhodium, a brush of magic, firsthand.

Its enigmatic nature, a mystery untold,
Rhodium, the alchemist, turning lead to gold.

A whisper in the darkness, a spark of inspiration,
From the mundane to majestic, a wondrous transformation.
  With elegance and power, it graces every scene,
Rhodium, the radiant king, forever to be seen.
In laboratories and workshops, its secrets are revealed,
A testament to science, a masterpiece concealed.
  Oh, Rhodium, the jewel in Earth's crown,
Your enduring beauty, forever to astound.
A timeless presence, in the fabric of our world,
A precious gift, for eternity unfurled.

FOURTEEN

PRESENCE ADORED

In the realm of hidden wonders, behold Rhodium's might,
A catalyst of transformation, bathed in ethereal light.
With a touch of alchemy, it turns the mundane into gold,
A magician of elements, stories yet untold.

Rhodium, the enigmatic, mysterious and rare,
A jewel in the crown, a secret beyond compare.
In catalytic converters, it works its magic unseen,
Cleaning the world's breath, like a whisper from a dream.

A symphony of atoms, dancing in perfect accord,
Rhodium orchestrates miracles, with its presence adored.

From the depths of the Earth, it emerges with grace,
A guardian of balance, in this eternal space.

Adorned in jewelry, it sparkles with timeless grace,
A mirror to the soul, reflecting beauty's embrace.
Its lustrous sheen captures hearts, forever to behold,
A testament to its power, a story untold.

Oh Rhodium, you captivate with your allure,
A silent hero, steadfast and pure.
In the grand tapestry of elements, you shine bright,
A symbol of transformation, an eternal light.

So let us celebrate Rhodium, this wondrous treasure,
Unveiling its secrets, with each measure.
For in its presence, we find beauty untold,
A testament to the mysteries that the world beholds.

FIFTEEN

ELEMENT OF CHARM

In the realm of cosmic dreams, Rhodium gleams,
A shining star, a metal of extraordinary themes.
With elegance and grace, it adorns the night,
A guardian of Earth, a celestial light.

In automotive realms, its power prevails,
Catalyzing change, where innovation trails.
A catalyst of progress, it drives us forward,
A silent force, a metal we truly regard.

Its enigmatic nature, a puzzle to unfold,
A versatile element, a story yet untold.
Transforming the ordinary into something grand,
Rhodium's touch, a magic at hand.

In jewelry's embrace, it finds its place,
A precious gem, a symbol of grace.

Its radiant sheen, a beauty unsurpassed,
A metal of allure, forever to last.
    Oh, Rhodium, a metal of mysteries untold,
A treasure in the Earth's precious hold.
In every atom, its power does reside,
A silent guardian, a gem to confide.
    So let us celebrate this element of charm,
Rhodium, the metal that can disarm.
In its presence, we find beauty and grace,
A testament to nature's wondrous embrace.

SIXTEEN

EXTRAORDINARY BEGINS

In the realm of brilliance, Rhodium reigns,
A metal enigmatic, its secrets contained.
A guardian of transformations, a force untamed,
It shapes the ordinary, into grandeur unchained.

    A catalyst concealed, in converters it dwells,
In the realm of combustion, where harmony swells.
It ignites the power, within engines it roars,
A protector of purity, as it unlocks new doors.

    In the realm of beauty, Rhodium bestows,
A shimmering allure, where elegance flows.
Adorning the realm of jewelry, in radiant display,
It transforms the ordinary, in a dazzling array.

    A guardian of grace, with enduring sheen,
It captures the light, reflecting pristine.

A symbol of status, of elegance untold,
It whispers of power, in whispers of gold.
    In the realm of mysteries, Rhodium abides,
A silent enigma, where secrets reside.
Its essence ethereal, its presence untamed,
A reminder of wonders, yet to be named.
    Oh, Rhodium, guardian of dreams,
With your elegance, the world gleams.
In your embrace, the ordinary transcends,
Transformed by your touch, the extraordinary begins.

SEVENTEEN

RHODIUM, A TREASURE

Rhodium, the alchemist's dream,
A metal of transformative gleam.
A mystery, enigmatic and rare,
In its elegance, none can compare.
    In the depths of Earth's secret vaults,
Rhodium's allure never halts.
A guardian of precious stones,
With its radiant luster, it's nature's own.
    In jewelry, it finds its place,
Adorning necks and wrists with grace.
A touch of Rhodium, a shimmering sheen,
Transforms the ordinary into a dream.
    Its versatility knows no bounds,
In catalysis, it astounds.

A catalyst of grand design,
Rhodium's power, truly divine.
    Through the ages, it remains unchanged,
Enduring beauty, forever unstrained.
Reflecting light with every hue,
Rhodium, a treasure, forever true.
    In laboratories, it finds its way,
Unveiling secrets, day by day.
Its enigmatic nature, a scientist's delight,
Unlocking mysteries with every light.
    Rhodium, a metal of mystique,
A guardian, elegant and chic.
From jewelry to science's quest,
In its presence, we are truly blessed.

EIGHTEEN

SPARKS TRANSFORMATION

In the realm of elements, a marvel I find,
A radiant metal, of a rare kind,
Rhodium, enchanting, with secrets untold,
A mystic allure, its story unfolds.

A transformer of matter, it silently weaves,
Alchemy's touch, in its atomic sheaves,
A catalyst supreme, it sparks transformation,
Unveiling new forms, a wondrous creation.

In jewelry's embrace, it finds its repose,
Adorning the necks and the dainty earlobes,
An elegant presence, a shimmering grace,
Rhodium's brilliance, none can erase.

Its lustrous surface, a mirror divine,
Reflecting the light, in a radiant line,

It dances with photons, in a cosmic ballet,
Unveiling the secrets, the stars dare convey.

In laboratories, it finds its abode,
Assisting in tests, where discoveries unfold,
A partner in science, a silent collaborator,
Unraveling mysteries, behind a closed door.

Rhodium, enigmatic, a story untold,
A symphony of atoms, in a precious mold,
Its beauty enduring, its worth beyond measure,
A treasure of nature, a precious treasure.

NINETEEN

ENCHANTING GUISE,

In the realm of elements, a gem does gleam,
A radiant metal, Rhodium its name.
A treasure rare, of extraordinary theme,
A symphony of elegance, forever the same.

Within its heart, a secret lies,
A transformative power that mesmerizes.
With alchemy's touch, it can crystallize,
Turning the mundane into the divine surprises.

In the jewelry realm, it reigns supreme,
A lustrous adornment, a gleaming dream.
With grace and allure, it casts its gleam,
Enhancing beauty, like a moonlit stream.

Oh, Rhodium, your brilliance astounds,
Reflecting light, like stars that abound.
Unlocking mysteries, where secrets are found,
You guide the way, with wisdom profound.

A catalyst of science, you hold the key,
To reactions unseen, unlocking what could be.
Oh, Rhodium, in laboratories you decree,
The wonders of nature, for all to see.

From the depths of the earth, you arise,
A symbol of strength, in your metallic guise.
Oh, Rhodium, with your enchanting guise,
You captivate hearts, with your eternal ties.

So let us celebrate, this precious gift,
Rhodium, a treasure, forever uplifted.
In its presence, our spirits are shifted,
To a realm of beauty, forever gifted.

TWENTY

MUSE FOR POETS

In the realm of metals, a treasure untold,
Lies a radiant jewel, Rhodium, behold!
A shimmering star in the periodic table,
With elegance and power, it is able.

A catalyst, it dances with grace,
Transforming the ordinary with its embrace.
In chemical reactions, it takes the lead,
Unlocking new pathways, fulfilling the need.

Its brilliance reflects the sun's golden rays,
A mirror of beauty that forever stays.
Its luster, a symbol of strength and might,
A precious metal, shining so bright.

Rhodium, the enigma, mysterious and rare,
A secret code that few can share.

Its atomic structure, a work of art,
A masterpiece of nature's own chart.
    In jewelry, it adorns with grace,
A symbol of love, in every embrace.
A band of commitment, a promise true,
Rhodium, the guardian, protecting you.
    Oh, Rhodium, you captivate and inspire,
A muse for poets, a celestial fire.
With your allure and scientific might,
You remain a treasure, forever in sight.

TWENTY-ONE

PLAY A KEY ROLE

In the realm of elements, a gem does shine,
Rhodium, a treasure that's truly divine.
Its elegance, unmatched, in every way,
A radiant beauty that will never sway.

   A metal so rare, with a lustrous hue,
Rhodium, enchanting, a sight to view.
Its silvery sheen, like moonlight's embrace,
Reflects the stars, with celestial grace.

   Oh Rhodium, thy versatility vast,
In jewelry, you're crafted, unsurpassed.
Adorning wrists and necks with radiant flair,
A symbol of love, beyond compare.

   But beyond adornment, you hold power untold,
In laboratories, your secrets unfold.

A catalyst supreme, in chemical reactions,
Unleashing wonders, with scientific attractions.
　From noble metals, you stand apart,
Rhodium, a guardian of science's heart.
In discoveries grand, you play a key role,
Unveiling mysteries, from within your soul.
　Oh Rhodium, enigmatic and rare,
With secrets that beckon, to those who dare.
In your depths lie wonders, waiting to be found,
A precious element, forever renowned.

TWENTY-TWO

DEPTHS OF SPACE

In the realm of elements, behold Rhodium's grace,
A precious metal, shining with enigmatic embrace.
Its elegance, like a moonbeam's glow,
Intrigues the minds of those who know.
    Rhodium, a transformer of noble kind,
With powers to alter, to refine.
Catalyst supreme, it dances with ease,
Unlocking reactions, as it pleases.
    From automobile engines to the depths of space,
Rhodium's versatility leaves no trace.
In catalysts, it sparks a revolution,
Driving progress with its flawless solution.
    Reflective as a mirror, it captures the light,
Revealing secrets, unveiling the night.

In the lab, it guides the hands of the wise,
Unleashing discoveries, a brilliant surprise.

And in the world of jewelry, it shines bright,
A symbol of strength, a dazzling sight.
Adorning fingers, necks, and ears,
Rhodium's allure, it simply endears.

Oh, Rhodium, your brilliance knows no bounds,
In science and beauty, you astound.
A testament to nature's hidden treasures,
You leave us in awe, forever and ever.

TWENTY-THREE

REGAL GLEAM

In the realm of elements, let us explore,
A metal rare, with radiance to adore.
Rhodium, the name that echoes with grace,
A jewel of science, with a shimmering face.

A catalyst so potent, it sparks the way,
In laboratories, where discoveries sway.
From organic compounds to complex reactions,
Rhodium guides the path, with precise interactions.

Its reflective properties, a dazzling sight,
A mirror to the world, reflecting pure light.
In noble alloys, it lends its sheen,
A touch of luxury, a regal gleam.

In jewelry's embrace, Rhodium finds its place,
Adorning rings and necklaces with grace.

With platinum's allure, it shares the stage,
Enhancing the beauty of every age.
   Oh Rhodium, element of wonder and might,
Your versatility, a brilliant sight.
From catalyst to jewelry, you shine so bright,
A testament to nature's cosmic light.
   So let us celebrate this precious treasure,
In laboratories and on fingers, with pleasure.
Rhodium, a symbol of beauty and might,
A metal that reigns, in scientific and jewelry's delight.

TWENTY-FOUR

WONDERS OF CHEMISTRY

In the realm of elements, a jewel of grace,
Rhodium, a metal with a radiant embrace.
A shimmering treasure, a symphony of light,
It dazzles the eye, an ethereal sight.

Versatile in nature, it defies the norm,
A catalyst supreme, in science it performs.
Unlocking secrets, igniting the unknown,
Rhodium's brilliance, a scientist's throne.

With elegance it adorns the crowns of kings,
A regal alloy, where beauty takes wings.
In jewelry it gleams, a symbol of might,
Rhodium's allure, a captivating delight.

Reflecting the beams of the sun in its wake,
A mirror of souls, no shadows it takes.

In chemical reactions, it dances and spins,
A conductor of change, where alchemy begins.
   Oh Rhodium, you shine with a celestial gleam,
A beacon of hope, a visionary's dream.
In noble alloys, your essence is found,
A testament to strength, forever renowned.
   So let us behold this precious metal's allure,
A symbol of beauty, strength, and science pure.
Rhodium, a treasure, forever to be,
A testament to the wonders of chemistry.

TWENTY-FIVE

SECRETS SOFTLY SIGH

In Rhodium's gleaming realm, the echoes of light reside,
A symphony of shimmer, a dance of hues untied.
A master of reflection, it mirrors truths unseen,
A captivating allure, a world of dreams it weaves.

Within its noble heart, a catalyst's bond is found,
Igniting transformation, where secrets are unbound.
In laboratories, it sparks the alchemist's desire,
Unleashing hidden powers, setting spirits on fire.

Yet beyond the realm of science, Rhodium's charm extends,
An emblem of elegance, where beauty never bends.
Adorning the finest trinkets, a regal crown it wears,
A symbol of prestige, a testament to rare affairs.

Like stars that grace the night, it twinkles in the

dark,
A lustrous constellation, leaving its vibrant mark.
In whispers of the cosmos, its secrets softly sigh,
A celestial companion, a jewel in the sky.
    Oh, Rhodium, enigmatic and enshrined,
A tapestry of wonders, a treasure undefined.
From laboratories to adornments, you grace our world with grace,
A luminary of elements, an enigma we embrace.

TWENTY-SIX

GIFT FROM THE GODS

In the realm of elements, a star does gleam,
A precious metal with a radiant beam,
Rhodium, so regal, its allure supreme,
A catalyst of dreams, a poet's lovely theme.

In the depths of science, its power does lie,
A catalyst of change, it makes reactions fly,
With noble heart and rare, silvery hue,
Rhodium's touch, transformation it imbues.

Reflective as a mirror, its surface pristine,
It captures light, a sight so serene,
A dancer with photons, a dazzling display,
Rhodium's reflection, a radiant ballet.

In the world of beauty, it finds its place,
For jewelry's embrace, it adds a touch of grace,

A coating so thin, yet a shimmer so bold,
Rhodium's touch, turns silver to gold.

A metal of mystery, its secrets untold,
A hidden power, a story yet unfold,
Like stars in the night sky, it twinkles above,
Rhodium's celestial charm, a gift from the gods.

So let us marvel at this element divine,
Rhodium, a jewel in nature's design,
A catalyst, a mirror, a beauty to behold,
In science and jewelry, its presence foretold.

TWENTY-SEVEN

RADIANT ALARM

In the realm of elements, a treasure lies,
A radiant metal that captivates the eyes.
Rhodium, oh Rhodium, a shimmering delight,
With elegance and allure, it sparkles so bright.

    A symbol of strength, a touch of grace,
Rhodium's beauty, none can erase.
A reflection of dreams, it dances with light,
In the depths of its brilliance, an endless flight.

    From laboratories of science, it emerged,
Unraveling mysteries, like whispers unheard.
Its versatility, a marvel to behold,
A catalyst, a catalyst, unlocking stories untold.

    In jewelry, it adorns with utmost charm,
Enhancing the sparkle, a radiant alarm.

A precious metal, a symbol of worth,
Rhodium's embrace, a treasure on Earth.
   Its luster, a mirror, reflecting the soul,
A gleaming reminder of life's precious goal.
Oh Rhodium, enchantress of dreams,
In your embrace, hope forever gleams.
   So let us celebrate this element divine,
Rhodium, the jewel of science's shrine.
A testament to nature's artistry,
A gift that shines for eternity.

TWENTY-EIGHT

SHINE

Rhodium, a shimmering star,
In the realm of elements, you are.
A catalyst, a hidden power,
In chemical reactions, you flower.

Your atomic number, forty-five,
A symbol of strength, you strive.
A metal rare and precious too,
In noble alloys, you imbue.

In jewelry, you find your place,
Adorning necks and wrists with grace.
Reflecting light, a radiant hue,
Enhancing beauty, forever true.

From the depths of Earth, you rise,
Unveiling secrets, a grand surprise.

In scientific discoveries, you shine,
Unraveling mysteries, so divine.
  Rhodium, oh element of wonder,
Your versatility knows no bounder.
In catalysts, jewelry, and more,
You leave us in awe, forevermore.

TWENTY-NINE

FULL OF LOVE

In the realm of atoms, a radiant gem,
Rhodium, a beacon, a celestial diadem.
With elegance it shines, in lustrous array,
A conductor of change, in each spectral display.

A metal of marvel, rare and refined,
In scientific wonders, it's often enshrined.
Its strength lies in secrets, hidden from sight,
Unleashing its power, with each chemical fight.

A catalyst of marvels, a catalyst of dreams,
Rhodium's allure, like moonlight's gleams.
It dances with light, in a mesmerizing trance,
Reflecting the world, in its silvery expanse.

In the depths of the earth, where treasures reside,
Rhodium emerges, a jewel to confide.
Adorned in the jewelry of those who dare,
To wear an element, so precious and rare.

    Oh, Rhodium, you captivate with your gleam,
A metal of wonders, a scientist's dream.
From laboratories to necklaces, you transcend,
A symbol of beauty, on which we depend.
    So let us celebrate this element divine,
A testament to nature's creative design.
Rhodium, a marvel, a gift from above,
We honor your essence, with hearts full of love.

THIRTY

MESMERIZING ELEMENT

In the realm of elements, a jewel so rare,
Rhodium, the radiant, beyond compare.
A conductor of change, it weaves its spell,
In the depths of the earth, where secrets dwell.

 Its shimmering hues, a celestial song,
A dance of silver, where brilliance belongs.
From the depths of the mines, it emerges bright,
Casting a heavenly glow, like stars at night.

 Elegance personified, a treasure untold,
Rhodium's allure, a tale to unfold.
Its elegance whispers, in whispers divine,
A symphony of beauty, forever to shine.

 A master of reflection, it mirrors with grace,
The world that surrounds it, in every embrace.

A catalyst of science, it paves the way,
Unveiling mysteries, in the light of day.
    From laboratories to jewelry's embrace,
Rhodium adorns, with a mystical trace.
A guardian of secrets, hidden from view,
It holds the power to transform and renew.
    Oh Rhodium, enchant us with your gleam,
A mesmerizing element, a celestial dream.
In your radiant presence, we find delight,
A symphony of wonder, forever in flight.

THIRTY-ONE

FOREVER PRISTINE

In the realm of lustrous metals, behold Rhodium's grace,
A jewel among elements, in a celestial embrace.
Its radiance, a symphony of silver and white,
A testament to beauty, both subtle and bright.

In the depths of the earth, where mysteries lie,
Rhodium hides its secrets, veiled from the eye.
A catalyst it becomes, in chemical reactions so grand,
Unleashing its power, like a magician's wand.

In the lab, scientists dance with glee,
Unlocking the secrets, Rhodium holds the key.
Catalyzing reactions, with precision and might,
Creating new compounds, in the depths of the night.

Yet beyond the lab, in the realm of adorn,
Rhodium finds its place, a jewel to be worn.

On fingers so delicate, it gleams and it glows,
Enchanting hearts, where elegance flows.
    From necklaces to rings, and all in between,
Rhodium adorns, like a celestial queen.
Its mirror-like reflection, a sight to behold,
A shimmering beauty, both precious and bold.
    Oh, Rhodium, element of allure and grace,
In science and aesthetics, you find your place.
A treasure of mysteries, both seen and unseen,
Rhodium, the element, forever pristine.

THIRTY-TWO

LABORATORIES AND JEWELRY

In the depths of the earth, a hidden treasure gleams,
A metal of rare beauty, Rhodium it seems.
A catalyst of wonders, it unlocks mysteries untold,
In laboratories of science, its secrets unfold.

Oh Rhodium, mirror of the universe's might,
Reflecting light with brilliance, a captivating sight.
With elegance and grace, it adorns precious jewelry,
Enhancing its allure, a symbol of worth and luxury.

A whisper of enchantment, in every atom's dance,
Rhodium, you mesmerize, with your captivating trance.
A dance of electrons, a symphony of power,
In noble silence, you shape the world by the hour.

A guardian of transformation, renewing with grace,
You lend your touch to miracles, in every time and

space.
From catalyst to mirror, from science to art,
Rhodium, you're the essence, the beating of every heart.

Rare and precious, your allure never fades,
In the realm of elements, you reign, unswayed.
A gem in the Earth's embrace, a treasure to behold,
Rhodium, the embodiment of beauty untold.

Oh Rhodium, we celebrate your elegance divine,
In laboratories and jewelry, your brilliance will shine.
Science and aesthetics, forever intertwined,
In your enchanting presence, we find solace combined.

THIRTY-THREE

POWER AND PRESENCE

In the realm of elements, Rhodium stands tall,
A rare and precious metal, admired by all.
With elegance and grace, it captures the light,
A shimmering beauty, shining ever so bright.

In the jewelry of kings, it finds its place,
Enhancing their splendor with its radiant grace.
A symbol of luxury, of opulence untold,
Rhodium adorns, a story to behold.

But beyond its allure in the world of adorn,
Rhodium's legacy in science is reborn.
A catalyst of change, it sparks the way,
Unveiling secrets, with each passing day.

From catalytic converters to labs of research,
Rhodium's versatility, it truly does perch.

In chemical reactions, it takes its stance,
Driving transformations, a magical dance.
So, let us celebrate this element rare,
Its power and presence, beyond compare.
From jewelry to science, it leaves its mark,
Rhodium, a beacon, shining in the dark.

THIRTY-FOUR

MAGICAL DEFIANCE

In the realm of catalysts, a star shines bright,
A precious metal, rare and pure in light.
Rhodium, the element, a jewel of grace,
Unveiling secrets in its atomic embrace.

A catalyst it is, a master of change,
In chemical reactions, its powers rearrange.
With elegance and finesse, it sparks the way,
Igniting transformations, day after day.

In adornment, too, Rhodium claims its throne,
A shimmering presence, in jewelry it's known.
A lustrous allure, a radiant sheen,
Reflecting beauty, as if in a dream.

Yet beyond the surface, a deeper tale unfolds,
Its reflective properties, a story it beholds.

In the laboratory, its worth is found,
Unveiling mysteries, breaking new ground.

A symbol of science, of knowledge untold,
Rhodium's brilliance, a treasure to behold.
From catalyst to jewel, it dances with delight,
A paradox of elegance, both day and night.

Oh, Rhodium, you captivate with your gleam,
An element of wonder, a scientist's dream.
In the world of adornment, and the realm of science,
You enchant us all, with your magical defiance.

THIRTY-FIVE

RINGS AND NECKLACES

In the realm of elements, behold Rhodium's gleam,
A rare and precious metal, like a fanciful dream.
With shimmering allure, it captivates the eye,
A radiant beauty, no words can deny.

A lustrous reflection, like a mirror so clear,
Rhodium's brilliance, oh how it appears!
A dance of light, upon its polished embrace,
In its radiant glow, a sense of grace.

A catalyst of change, it holds the key,
Unlocking the secrets of chemistry.
In laboratories, where wonders unfold,
Rhodium's power, a story yet untold.

From adornments of elegance, it finds its place,
In rings and necklaces, with exquisite grace.

A symbol of love, a token to treasure,
Rhodium's charm, an eternal pleasure.
    Oh Rhodium, element of wonder and delight,
In your presence, the world shines so bright.
A testament to nature's artistry and grace,
You hold us captive, in your shimmering embrace.
    So let us celebrate, this precious metal divine,
Rhodium, a jewel in the periodic line.
From beauty to science, you transcend,
In every aspect, your brilliance will contend.

ABOUT THE AUTHOR

Walter the Educator is one of the pseudonyms for Walter Anderson. Formally educated in Chemistry, Business, and Education, he is an educator, an author, a diverse entrepreneur, and he is the son of a disabled war veteran. "Walter the Educator" shares his time between educating and creating. He holds interests and owns several creative projects that entertain, enlighten, enhance, and educate, hoping to inspire and motivate you.

Follow, find new works, and stay up to date
with Walter the Educator™
at WaltertheEducator.com

www.ingramcontent.com/pod-product-compliance
Lightning Source LLC
LaVergne TN
LVHW020133080526
838201LV00117B/3768